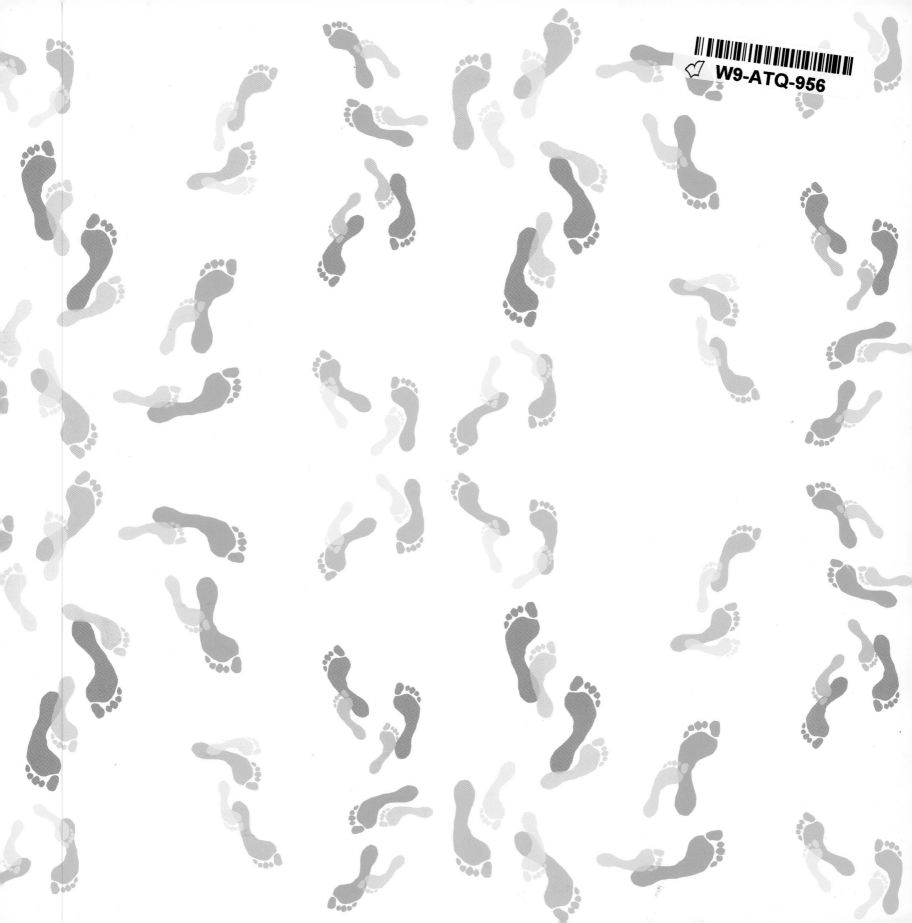

Concordia Publishing House

3558 South Jefferson Avenue, St. Louis, MO 63118-3968
Copyright © 2000 Ottenheimer Publishers, Inc.

Cover and interior design by Susan L. Chamberlain

Printed in China
ISBN 0-570-07035-X
SB654MLKJIHGFEDCBA

In His Footsteps

Written by Cathy Drinkwater Better

Illustrated by Elena Kucharik

Concordia Publishing House

I will think of God's love for His children,

And remember how much He loves me.

I will walk in the footsteps of Jesus,
And be the best friend I can be.

When someone says things that can hurt me,

Or laughs at me and leaves me to cry,

I will walk in the footsteps of Jesus,

Forgive him, and never ask why.

If I see someone hungry or thirsty,

Or someone who is cold and alone,

I will walk in the footsteps of Jesus,
And share with her all that I own.

So many feel pain and know sorrow.

So many have worries and fears.

I will walk in the footsteps of Jesus,
Give comfort, and help dry their tears.

God sent His dear Son, Jesus,

To bring peace, love, and joy to us all.

We can walk in the footsteps of Jesus,

No matter how big or how small.

God helps me walk in His footsteps,

Helps me love everyone whom I see.

I will walk in the footsteps of Jesus.

Take my hand, and walk there with me.